A Wonderful World Of Poems

Shanaya Suraj Agarwal

BookLeaf Publishing

India | USA | UK

Made with ❤ on the BookLeaf Publishing Platform
www.bookleafpub.in
www.bookleafpub.com

Dedication

These fun, wonky, and memorable poems were only possible because of

My kind, loving and supporting mother, who was always standing by me, who never lets me down, and who had my back all throughout this adventurous creative writing journey, a very special thanks to you Mumma for always believing in me no matter what so this book is for you.

My BFF, Anya, who always stands up for me and who is the sun in my rainy day, thank you for doing all you have done for me I am super grateful, I always love hanging out with you and wish to be your twin sister. Again, thank you a lot!

A person who is a mix of teaching, motherly feel, and friendliness (who is also Anya's mother) Jaya aunty, thanks for always making me feel at home whenever I am with you and thank you for all you have done for me, I have dedicated this book to you, Anya, and my mother.

Thanks a lot for all you guys have done for me, I really appreciate this and am very grateful. Thanks a lot again!

Preface

Once there was a time when my mother didn't speak much.She hardly smiled and laughed, it was like darkness, but still she loved and protected us with all her might. I couldn't understand what was going on in her mind, so I started writing about her feelings.I enjoyed writing, it opened a new chapter in my life and writing poems took me to my happy place so, eventually thought about entering a 21 poem challenge and here I am, writing it right now.

These poems will take you to the ride of different emotions, feelings and to different world altogether. Hope you enjoy the ride.

Acknowledgements

I want to thank Shradha ma'am, Shikha ma'am, and Pranjal ma'am for encouraging me write these poems.

1. When Mummy Is Happy

When my mother is happy,
She is as sweet as honey,
She becomes very yappy,
Sometimes she gets a bit sappy,
She gets a bit snappy,
But her laughter dances like a sunny,
Whirlwind of joy, never too crummy,
In her embrace, worries feel puny,
For in her smile, life blooms, so lovely.

2. When Mummy Is Sad

When my mother is sad,
She gets a bit mad,
I miss all the times she was rad,
When we used to watch movies on my iPad,
When she would not be mad,
When she didn't get sad.

3. My Mother's Exciting Times

When my mother is excited,
Once her ice-cream went splat,
She made a chapati super flat,
She also saw a cute baby bat,
And on the grass she sat,
Under the sun where the daisies chat,
With a laugh that could soothe a tired cat,
She danced around in her colorful hat,
her joy so big, it made time feel like a vat.

4. What I Think Of My Mother And What She Thinks Of Me

My mother thinks I am cranky,
Because I can't find my blanky,
My mother gets a bit sassy,
While I think she is classy,
I doubt she knows the meaning of wacky,
In our world where silly feels not so tacky.

5. Mumma Likes To Laugh

My mother loves to laugh,
And she is not a cleaning staff,
She knows how to solve a graph,
She cuts her brownies in half,
She longs to have a cook off,
As joy and baking share the aftermath.

6. Rainy Days

It rains almost every day,
Which makes the world sad and gloomy,
But it can sometimes be fun,
When you dance around and play,
That parts fun, but not when it gets cold,
Because when it's cold you can catch a cold or maybe
even fever which is worse,
But the important thing is that you have fun,
Because fun is fun.

7. The Tundra Biome

The tundra biome is cold,
Though it doesn't seem too old,
Every second its beauty seems to unfold,
I think its uniqueness is just bold,
It might hold some kind of gold,
Do you think its uniqueness should fold?
Well, I certainly don't.

8. My Most Favourite Thing In My Room

My most favourite thing in my room is,
A squishy named 'Tis Adventurous'
Though I wouldn't make a fuss,
Should I take her into a bus?
Well, I think she is generous,
Certainly not dangerous,
She helps me calm down when I am nervous,
Sometimes, I think its the world versus us.

9. My Version Of Friends

I think friends should be kind,
Someone who wouldn't mind,
Someone who you can find,
Someone who in some way wouldn't think you're blind,
Someone who thinks the both of you will bind,
Though someone who isn't fined?

10. Roses

Roses are red,
The meadows are swinging,
And how beautiful they smell!
Roses are my favourite types of flowers,
And how divine they look,
I love them so, so much,
I could never go a day without them in the winters,
That is why I have a rose bush growing in the backyard!

11. Daises

Daises are pearl white,
Their fragrance makes me want to forget about
everything that's happening around me,
So beautiful and delicate they are!
I love the way they look,
It's as if you are in a dream when you see them,
I would treat them as if they are my pets,
So super nicely and delicately,
I would never let them out of my sight.

12. The Grassland Biome

The grassland biome is so beautiful,
With all it's animals and plants,
I think that we should protect the wildlife with all our
might,
Who knows?
It's beauty might unfold in the evening,
The trees are giving a cry of help,
The animals are encouraging you to help hem save their
home,
They would love it if more hands came to help them,
Do you think that you will protect them with all your
might?
Well, I know that you will try.

13. Brothers

Brothers are brothers,
No matter what,
Sometimes they help you through hard times,
Sometimes they don't,
Sometimes they will give you things of your desire,
Sometimes they won't,
Sometimes they care for you,
Sometimes they don't,
But in the end,
They are the ones who care for you the most.

14. Best Friends

Best friends are people who stick by you and who love
you for the way that you are,
They won't judge you,
They won't make fun of you,
They will insult you just for fun but they won't mean it,
Best friends are people who might be a little rude to you,
Fake friends are people you are nice to you all the time
and who will leave you through hard times,
Best friends are the people who will stick by you no
matter what happens,
They will also help you through your hard times and
won't ever leave you,
At least that's what I think best friends are.

15. Nature

Nature isn't just animals and plants,
And natural disasters only happen because of nature,
When nature is sad, it makes a natural disaster that
represents that feeling,
When nature is happy, it might give sunlight all day,
When it wants to cry, it will give rain,
Sure, nature is beautiful, but it's about what calmness
represents because nature is calm unless you disturb it.

16. Books

Books make me want to go to another world for hours if
not days,
They keep me busy for at least a quarter of a day,
They also transport me to a different world,
They make me want to spend the whole day reading
only,
They help keep me busy every day because I have
nothing to do,
They brighten up my day for me,
It is such a nice thing that I something to keep me busy
every day!

17. My Naanu

My Naanu much dear,
Brings me so much joy and cheer,
He hugs so tight,
That I feel his warmth every night,
I know I'm the apple of his eye,
I would never tell him a lie,
His love for mangoes is immense,
He says everything that makes sense,
His craving for Aloo Bedmi is unstoppable,
My Naanu is the most loveable.

18. My Naani

The folktales of Naani are gold,
With hundreds of them untold,
Humanity is her forte,
We meet every Saturday,
Each tale of Naani is filled with sapience,
No one dares to question her cognizance,
She's the most helpful,
Her soul is beautifully colorful.

19. Addy Maamu

Addy Maamu is a magical blend,
Of fun and proficiency that never ends,
He gives me trivia which are mentally bright,
He never comes to stay for the night,
For soccer he has a soft spot,
He can solve any puzzle knot,
He illuminates what's self love,
He is as kind as a dove.

20. Strange Strangers

A lady driving a new car,
Thinking to not step into a messy bar.
A delivery boy driving a scootie,
Thinking to have a little frooti.
A man riding a bicycle,
Going home to take a nibble.
A gentleman on the road,
Paving the way for his little toad,
Strangers are strange,
They always change.

21. Hobbies

Yesterday I doodled for the first time,
Today in the morning I read a book called "The BFG",
I am planning to read autobiographies about people,
A month ago I started writing poems and entered the 21
poem writing challenge,
In May I am planning to celebrate my birthday,
About five years ago I developed my passion for reading,
Two years ago I developed my passion for visual arts,
Today I did karate and it was very fun.

www.ingramcontent.com/pod-product-compliance
Lightning Source LLC
LaVergne TN
LVHW051249200726
843510LV00011B/1764